Normal Healthy Patterns

Natural combinations of birth Personalities are: Popular Sanguine/Powerful Choleric, Powerful Choleric/Perfect Melancholy, Perfect Melancholy/Peaceful Phlegmatic, and Peaceful Phlegmatic/Popular Sanguine. One of the two will be your dominant Personality and the other will be your secondary Personality. Most everyone has a dominant and a secondary Personality, but the numbers may vary greatly. For example, if you scored 32 Powerful Choleric and 8 Perfect Melancholy, you would be described as a very strong Powerful Choleric with some Perfect Melancholy traits. However, it is also quite possible to have more evenly balanced scores in two columns. A few checks in the remaining two columns can generally be ignored as insignificant. Any test such as this can be assumed to have a 10 percent margin of error, for the words simply represent how you perceive yourself. Normal healthy patterns are usually characterized by similar and balancing scores of strengths and weaknesses in any single column.

Unnatural Combinations

There are two combinations that are not natural (although often seen): Popular Sanguine/Perfect Melancholy and Powerful Choleric/Peaceful Phlegmatic. Either of these two combinations is evidence of either a misunderstanding or a Personality mask, as they are diametrically opposed to each other and are not natural birth Personality combinations. To determine your true Personality, review the Profile again. First, make sure that you used the word definitions for each and every selection, and be sure that you selected the words that represent your true, natural self before you worked at becoming a more mature, better person. For example, if you are organized—but it is something that you have made a conscious effort to achieve rather than something you have been all your life—do not check "Orderly." Basically, if you have "learned" it, do not check it. Second, go back over each grouping of words. If you had a difficult time choosing between two words, check both words. If none of the words seemed appropriate, skip that line. While this approach will adjust the totals so that they do not add up to the usual 40, it will give a more accurate profile and usually clears up any confusion on the Personality pattern. If this approach still produces an unnatural combination, it may be indicative of a Personality mask. Personality masks are typically the result of outside forces working in a person's life to make him or her conform to someone else's concept of who he or she should be, or they could be something the individual put on in childhood to survive in a difficult or dysfunctional family living situation. For more information on "misunderstandings" and/or "masking," read *Wired That Way*.

Causes of Masking

1. A domineering parent or one with unrealistic expectations can cause masking when he or she constantly requires the child to conform to Personality traits that are not natural to the child.
2. Living in a home with alcoholism, severe illness, or extreme dysfunction may cause unnatural pressures on a minor, dependent child to perform or contribute to the household, often assuming a parental role.
3. Strong feelings of rejection masking when a child does both parents. The child will often try to become whatever it takes to win attention and approval.
4. Some forms of emotional or physical abuse may lead to the child conforming to the demands of the abusing parent in hopes of stopping the harsh treatment.
5. Childhood sexual interference or violation, particularly when perpetrated by a parent or person in a parental role, may cause the child to adopt behaviors not natural to his or her Personality.
6. Growing up in a single-parent home might result in some form of Personality masking, especially if the child is firstborn, in which case the child may fulfill some of the roles of the absent parent.
7. Legalistic religious homes or those with intense regulatory standards can stifle a child's natural Personality.
8. A domineering or overly controlling spouse/partner or someone in a position of authority in adult life can also result in Personality masking as a form of coping or survival.
9. Adult abuse or rejection in marriage (or significant relationships) will often have some effect in distorting the natural Personality, as the lonely or hurting person simply gives up.

Combination of Three

For the reasons described above, any combination of three Personalities indicates that one must be a mask. Generally, the center of the three is the natural Personality, and one of the ends is the mask. For example, for a person scoring relatively evenly in Popular Sanguine/Powerful Choleric/Perfect Melancholy, the Powerful Choleric is generally the natural Personality, while either the Popular Sanguine or the Perfect Melancholy is the mask, as you were not born with both. Try to determine which is the mask. Frequently, a person who knows you well can objectively review your two columns in question and help you select the word that they feel describes you best. Or you can think back to how you would have answered before life's experiences distorted your perception of yourself, or at a time when you are your most comfortable with yourself. Such a review of the words you selected will frequently transfer enough of them to another column to clearly define your correct and natural birth Personalities.

Combination of Four

If your Profile scores are fairly even across all four categories, there are two possibilities as to why this has occurred. The first is that you really don't know yourself, you don't care, or you may be a Peaceful Phlegmatic who simply has trouble making choices. The second possibility (very rare) is that you are double-masked—the way that you perceive yourself has been so distorted by your life experiences that you don't really know who you are. Remember, it takes a great deal of energy to wear masks and live in Personality roles that are not naturally yours. The goal should be to take off the masks and live your life in the manner in which you were created.

PERSONALITY PROFILE WORD DEFINITIONS

1

Adventurous. Will take on new and daring enterprises with a determination to master them.
Adaptable. Easily fits in and is comfortable in any situation.
Animated. Full of life; lively use of hand, arm, and face gestures.
Analytical. Likes to examine the parts for their logical and proper relationships.

2

Persistent. Sees one project through to its completion before starting another.
Playful. Full of fun and good humor.
Persuasive. Convinces through logic and fact rather than charm or power.
Peaceful. Seems undisturbed and tranquil and retreats from any form of strife.

3

Submissive. Easily accepts any other's point of view or desire with little need to assert his or her own opinion.
Self-sacrificing. Willingly gives up his or her own personal being for the sake of or to meet the needs of others.
Sociable. Sees being with others as an opportunity to be cute and entertaining rather than as a challenge or business opportunity.
Strong-willed. Determined to have one's own way.

4

Considerate. Having regard for the needs and feelings of others.
Controlled. Has emotional feelings but rarely displays them.
Competitive. Turns every situation, happening, or game into a contest and always plays to win!
Convincing. Can win others over to anything through the sheer charm of his or her personality.

5

Refreshing. Renews and stimulates or makes others feel good.
Respectful. Treats others with deference, honor, and esteem.
Reserved. Self-restrained in expression of emotion or enthusiasm.
Resourceful. Able to act quickly and effectively in virtually all situations.

6

Satisfied. Easily accepts any circumstance or situation.
Sensitive. Intensively cares about others and what happens.
Self-reliant. Independent and can fully rely on his or her own capabilities, judgment, and resources.
Spirited. Full of life and excitement.

7

Planner. Prefers to work out a detailed arrangement beforehand for the accomplishment of a project or goal and prefers involvement with the planning stages and the finished product rather than the carrying out of the task.
Patient. Unmoved by delay, remains calm and tolerant.
Positive. Knows it will turn out right if he or she is in charge.
Promoter. Urges or compels others to go along, join, or invest through the charm of his or her own personality.

8

Sure. Confident, rarely hesitates or wavers.
Spontaneous. Prefers all of life to be impulsive, unpremeditated activity, not restricted by plans.
Scheduled. Makes and lives according to a daily plan; dislikes his or her plan to be interrupted.
Shy. Quiet, doesn't easily instigate a conversation.

9

Orderly. Has a methodical, systematic arrangement of things.
Obliging. Accommodating, is quick to do it another's way.
Outspoken. Speaks frankly and without reserve.
Optimistic. Sunny disposition who convinces self and others that everything will turn out all right.

10

Friendly. A responder rather than an initiator, seldom starts a conversation.
Faithful. Consistently reliable, steadfast, loyal and devoted, sometimes beyond reason.
Funny. Sparkling sense of humor that can make virtually any story into a hilarious event.
Forceful. A commanding personality whom others would hesitate to take a stand against.

11

Daring. Willing to take risks, fearless, bold.
Delightful. Is upbeat and fun to be with.
Diplomatic. Deals with people tactfully, sensitively, and patiently.
Detailed. Does everything in proper order with a clear memory of all the things that happen.

12

Cheerful. Consistently in good spirits and promoting happiness in others.

Consistent. Stays emotionally on an even keel, responding as one might expect.

Cultured. Interests involve both intellectual and artistic pursuits, such as theater, symphony, ballet.

Confident. Self-assured and certain of own ability and success.

13

Idealistic. Visualizes things in their perfect form and has a need to measure up to that standard himself or herself.

Independent. Self-sufficient, self-supporting, self-confident, and seems to have little need of help.

Inoffensive. Never says or causes anything unpleasant or objectionable.

Inspiring. Encourages others to work, join, or be involved, and makes the whole thing fun.

14

Demonstrative. Openly expresses emotion, especially affection, and doesn't hesitate to touch others while speaking to them.

Decisive. Has quick, conclusive, judgment-making ability.

Dry humor. Exhibits "dry wit," usually one-liners that can be sarcastic in nature.

Deep. Intense and often introspective with a distaste for surface conversation and pursuits.

15

Mediator. Consistently finds himself or herself in the role of reconciling differences in order to avoid conflict.

Musical. Participates in or has a deep appreciation for music; is committed to music as an art form rather than the fun of performance.

Mover. Driven by a need to be productive, is a leader whom others follow, finds it difficult to sit still.

Mixes easily. Loves a party and can't wait to meet everyone in the room; never meets a stranger.

16

Thoughtful. Considerate, remembers special occasions, and makes kind gestures.

Tenacious. Holds on firmly, stubbornly, and won't let go until the goal is accomplished.

Talker. Constantly talking, telling funny stories, and entertaining everyone around, feels need to fill silence in order to make others comfortable.

Tolerant. Easily accepts the thoughts and ways of others without the need to disagree with or change them.

17

Listener. Always seems willing to hear what others have to say.

Loyal. Faithful to a person, ideal, or job, sometimes beyond reason.

Leader. Is a natural-born director who is driven to be in charge and often finds it difficult to believe that anyone else can do the job as well.

Lively. Full of life, vigorous, energetic.

18

Contented. Easily satisfied with what he or she has, rarely envious.

Chief. Commands leadership and expects people to follow.

Chartmaker. Organizes life and tasks, making lists, forms, or graphs.

Cute. Precious, adorable, center of attention.

19

Perfectionist. Places high standards on himself or herself, and often on others, desiring that everything be in proper order at all times.

Pleasant. Easygoing, easy to be around, easy to talk with.

Productive. Must constantly be working or achieving, often finds it very difficult to rest.

Popular. Life of the party, and therefore much desired as a party guest.

20

Bouncy. A bubbly, lively personality, full of energy.

Bold. Fearless, daring, forward, unafraid of risk.

Behaved. Consistently desires to conduct himself or herself within the realm of what he or she feels is proper.

Balanced. Stable, middle-of-the-road personality, not subject to sharp highs or lows.

21

Blank. Shows little facial expression or emotion.

Bashful. Shrinks from getting attention, a result of his or her self-consciousness.

Brassy. Showy, flashy, comes on strong, too loud.

Bossy. Commanding, domineering, sometimes overbearing in adult relationships.

22

Undisciplined. Lack of order permeates most every area of his or her life.

Unsympathetic. Finds it difficult to relate to the problems or hurts of others.

Unenthusiastic. Tends to not get excited, often feeling it won't work anyway.

Unforgiving. Has difficulty forgiving or forgetting a hurt or injustice done to him or her, likely to hold on to a grudge.

23

Reticent. Unwilling or struggles against getting involved, especially when the situation is complex.

Resentful. Often holds ill feelings as a result of real or imagined offenses.

Resistant. Strives, works against or hesitates to accept any other way but his or her own.

Repetitious. Retells stories and incidents to entertain without realizing he or she has already told the story several times before, constantly needs to have something to say.

24

Fussy. Insistent over petty matters or details, calling for a great attention to trivial details.

Fearful. Often experiences feelings of deep concern, apprehension, or anxiousness.

Forgetful. Lack of memory, which is usually tied to a lack of discipline, and not bothering to mentally record things that aren't fun.

Frank. Straightforward, outspoken, and doesn't mind telling others exactly what he or she thinks.

25

Impatient. Finds it difficult to endure irritation or wait for others.

Insecure. Is apprehensive or lacks confidence.

Indecisive. Finds it difficult to make any decision at all (not the personality that labors long over each decision in order to make the perfect one).

Interrupts. Is more of a talker than a listener, starts speaking without even realizing someone else is already speaking.

26

Unpopular. Intensity and demand for perfection can push others away.

Uninvolved. Has no desire to listen or become interested in clubs, groups, activities, or other people's lives.

Unpredictable. May be ecstatic one moment and down the next, or willing to help but then disappears, or promises to come but forgets to show up.

Unaffectionate. Finds it difficult to verbally or physically demonstrate tenderness openly.

27

Headstrong. Insists on having his or her own way.

Haphazard. Has no consistent way of doing things.

Hard to please. Has standard set so high that it is difficult to ever satisfy him or her.

Hesitant. Slow to get moving and hard to get involved.

28

Plain. Has a middle-of-the-road personality without highs or lows and shows little, if any, emotion.

Pessimistic. Hopes for the best but generally sees the downside of a situation first.

Proud. Has great self-esteem and sees himself or herself as always right and the best person for the job.

Permissive. Allows others (including children) to do as they please in order to keep from being disliked.

29

Angered easily. Has a childlike flash-in-the-pan temper that expresses itself in tantrum style, which is over and forgotten almost instantly.

Aimless. Not a goal-setter and has little desire to be one.

Argumentative. Incites arguments because he or she is right, no matter what the situation may be.

Alienated. Easily feels estranged from others, often because of insecurity or fear that others don't really enjoy his or her company.

30

Naive. Simple and childlike perspective, lacking sophistication or comprehension of what the deeper levels of life are really about.

Negative attitude. Attitude is seldom positive and often able to see only the down or dark side of each situation.

Nervy. Full of confidence, fortitude, and sheer guts, often in a negative sense.

Nonchalant. Easygoing, unconcerned, indifferent.

31

Worrier. Consistently feels uncertain, troubled, or anxious.

Withdrawn. Pulls into himself or herself and needs a great deal of alone or isolation time.

Workaholic. An aggressive goal-setter who must be constantly productive and feels very guilty when resting, is not driven by a need for perfection or completion but by a need for accomplishment and reward.

Wants credit. Thrives on the credit or approval of others. As an entertainer, this person feeds on the applause, laughter, and/or acceptance of an audience.

32

Too sensitive. Overly introspective and easily offended when misunderstood.

Tactless. Sometimes expresses himself or herself in a somewhat offensive and inconsiderate way.

Timid. Shrinks from difficult situations.

Talkative. An entertaining, compulsive talker who finds it difficult to listen.

33

Doubtful. Characterized by uncertainty and lack of confidence that it will ever work out.

Disorganized. Lack of ability to ever get life in order.

Domineering. Compulsively takes control of situations and/or people, usually telling others what to do.

Depressed. Feels down much of the time.

34

Inconsistent. Erratic, contradictory, with actions and emotions not based on logic.

Introvert. A person whose thoughts and interests are directed inward, lives within himself or herself.

Intolerant. Appears unable to withstand or accept another's attitudes, point of view, or way of doing things.

Indifferent. Feels most things don't matter one way or the other.

35

Messy. Lives in a state of disorder, unable to find things.

Moody. Doesn't get very high emotionally but easily slips into low lows, often when feeling unappreciated.

Mumbles. Will talk quietly under his or her breath when pushed, doesn't bother to speak clearly.

Manipulative. Influences or manages shrewdly or deviously for his or her own advantage, will get his or her way somehow.

36

Slow. Doesn't often act or think quickly, too much of a bother.

Stubborn. Determined to exert his or her own will, not easily persuaded, obstinate.

Show-off. Needs to be the center of attention, wants to be watched.

Skeptical. Disbelieving, questioning the motive behind the words.

37

Loner. Requires a lot of private time and tends to avoid other people.

Lord over others. Doesn't hesitate to let others know that he or she is right or is in control.

Lazy. Evaluates work or activity in terms of how much energy it will take.

Loud. Has a laugh or voice that can be heard above others in the room.

38

Sluggish. Slow to get started, needs push to be motivated.

Suspicious. Tends to suspect or distrust others or ideas.

Short-tempered. Has a demanding impatience-based anger and a short fuse. Anger is expressed when others are not moving fast enough or have not completed what they have been asked to do.

Scatterbrained. Lacks the power of concentration or attention, flighty.

39

Revengeful. Knowingly or otherwise holds a grudge and punishes the offender, often by subtly withholding friendship or affection.

Restless. Likes constant new activity because it isn't fun to do the same things all the time.

Reluctant. Unwilling or struggles against getting involved.

Rash. May act hastily without thinking things through, generally because of impatience.

40

Compromising. Will often relax his or her position, even when right, in order to avoid conflict.

Critical. Constantly evaluating and making judgments, frequently thinking or expressing negative reactions.

Crafty. Shrewd, one who can always find a way to get to the desired end.

Changeable. A childlike, short attention span that needs a lot of change and variety to keep from getting bored.

PERSONALITY STRENGTHS AND WEAKNESSES

POPULAR SANGUINE

STRENGTHS

EMOTIONS
- Appealing personality
- Talkative, storyteller
- Good sense of humor
- Memory for color
- Physically hold on to listener
- Emotional and demonstrative
- Enthusiastic and expressive
- Cheerful and bubbling over
- Curious
- Good on stage
- Wide-eyed and innocent
- Lives in the present
- Changeable disposition
- Sincere at heart
- Always a child

WORK
- Volunteers for jobs
- Thinks up new activities
- Looks great on the surface
- Creative and colorful
- Has energy and enthusiasm
- Starts in a flashy way
- Inspires others to join
- Charms others to work

FRIENDS
- Makes friends easily
- Loves people
- Thrives on compliments
- Seems exciting
- Envied by others
- Doesn't hold grudges
- Apologizes quickly
- Prevents dull moments
- Likes spontaneous activities

WEAKNESSES

EMOTIONS
- Compulsive talker
- Exaggerates and elaborates
- Dwells on trivia
- Can't remember names
- Scares others off
- Too happy for some
- Has restless energy
- Egotistical
- Blusters and complains
- Naive, gets taken in
- Has loud voice and laugh
- Controlled by circumstances
- Gets angry easily
- Seems phony to some
- Never grows up

WORK
- Would rather talk
- Forgets obligations
- Doesn't follow through
- Confidence fades fast
- Undisciplined
- Priorities out of order
- Decides by feelings
- Easily distracted
- Wastes time talking

FRIENDS
- Hates to be alone
- Needs to be center stage
- Wants to be popular
- Looks for credit
- Dominates conversations
- Interrupts and doesn't listen
- Answers for others
- Fickle and forgetful
- Makes excuses
- Repeats stories

POWERFUL CHOLERIC

STRENGTHS

EMOTIONS
- Born leader
- Dynamic and active
- Compulsive need for change
- Must correct wrongs
- Strong-willed and decisive
- Unemotional
- Not easily discouraged
- Independent and self-sufficient
- Exudes confidence
- Can run anything

WORK
- Goal-oriented
- Sees the whole picture
- Organizes well
- Seeks practical solutions
- Moves quickly to action
- Delegates work
- Insists on production
- Makes the goal
- Stimulates activity
- Thrives on opposition

FRIENDS
- Has little need for friends
- Will work for group activity
- Will lead and organize
- Is usually right
- Excels in emergencies

WEAKNESSES

EMOTIONS
- Bossy
- Impatient
- Quick-tempered
- Can't relax
- Too impetuous
- Enjoys controversy and arguments
- Won't give up when losing
- Comes on too strong
- Inflexible
- Is not complimentary
- Dislikes tears and emotions
- Is unsympathetic

WORK
- Little tolerance for mistakes
- Doesn't analyze details
- Bored by trivia
- May make rash decisions
- May be rude or tactless
- Manipulates people
- Demanding of others
- End justifies the means
- Work may become his or her god
- Demands loyalty in the ranks

FRIENDS
- Tends to use people
- Dominates others
- Decides for others
- Knows everything
- Can do everything better
- Is too independent
- Possessive of friends and mate
- Can't say, "I'm sorry"
- May be right, but unpopular

PERFECT MELANCHOLY

STRENGTHS

EMOTIONS
- Deep and thoughtful
- Analytical
- Serious and purposeful
- Talented and creative
- Artistic or musical
- Philosophical and poetic
- Appreciative of beauty
- Sensitive to others
- Self-sacrificing
- Conscientious
- Idealistic

WORK
- Schedule-oriented
- Perfectionist, high standards
- Detail-conscious
- Persistent and thorough
- Orderly and organized
- Neat and tidy, economical
- Sees the problems
- Finds creative solutions
- Needs to finish what he or she starts
- Likes charts, graphs, figures, lists

FRIENDS
- Makes friends cautiously
- Content to stay in the background
- Avoids causing attention
- Faithful and devoted
- Will listen to complaints
- Can solve others' problems
- Deep concern for other people
- Moved to tears with compassion
- Seeks ideal mate

WEAKNESSES

EMOTIONS
- Remembers the negatives
- Moody and depressed
- Enjoys being hurt
- Has false humility
- Off in another world
- Low self-image
- Has selective hearing
- Self-centered
- Too introspective
- Guilt feelings
- Persecution complex
- Tends to hypochondria

WORK
- Not people-oriented
- Depressed over imperfections
- Chooses difficult work
- Hesitant to start projects
- Spends too much time planning
- Prefers analysis to work
- Self-deprecating
- Hard to please
- Standards often too high
- Deep need for approval

FRIENDS
- Lives through others
- Insecure socially
- Withdrawn and remote
- Critical of others
- Holds back affection
- Dislikes those in opposition
- Suspicious of people
- Antagonistic and vengeful
- Unforgiving
- Full of contradictions
- Skeptical of compliments

PEACEFUL PHLEGMATIC

STRENGTHS

EMOTIONS
- Low-key personality
- Easygoing and relaxed
- Calm, cool, and collected
- Patient, well-balanced
- Consistent life
- Quiet, but witty
- Sympathetic and kind
- Keeps emotions hidden
- Happily reconciled to life
- All-purpose person

WORK
- Competent and steady
- Peaceful and agreeable
- Has administrative ability
- Mediates problems
- Avoids conflicts
- Good under pressure
- Finds the easy way

FRIENDS
- Easy to get along with
- Pleasant and enjoyable
- Inoffensive
- Good listener
- Dry sense of humor
- Enjoys watching people
- Has many friends
- Has compassion and concern

WEAKNESSES

EMOTIONS
- Unenthusiastic
- Fearful and worried
- Indecisive
- Avoids responsibility
- Quiet will of iron
- Selfish
- Too shy and reticent
- Too compromising
- Self-righteous

WORK
- Not goal-oriented
- Lacks self-motivation
- Hard to get moving
- Resents being pushed
- Lazy and careless
- Discourages others
- Would rather watch

FRIENDS
- Dampens enthusiasm
- Stays uninvolved
- Is not exciting
- Indifferent to plans
- Judges others
- Sarcastic and teasing
- Resists change

PERSONALITY SCORING SHEET

Instructions

1

Now transfer all your *X*'s to the corresponding words on the Personality Scoring Sheet and add up your totals. For example, if you checked "Animated" on the Profile, check it on the Scoring Sheet to the right. (**Note:** The words are in a different order on the Profile and the Scoring Sheet.)

2

Tallying Your Score

Once you've transferred your answers to the Scoring Sheet, added up your total number of answers in each of the four columns, and added your totals from both the strengths and weaknesses sections, you'll know your dominant Personality type. You'll also know what combination you are. For example, if your score is 35 in Powerful Choleric strengths and weaknesses, there's really little question. You're almost all Powerful Choleric. But if your score is 16 in Powerful Choleric, 14 in Perfect Melancholy, and 5 in each of the others, you're a Powerful Choleric with strong Perfect Melancholy traits. Of course, you'll also know your least dominant type. You can read and work with your results in *Wired That Way*, the book that teaches you how to put your strengths to work, how to compensate for the weaknesses in your dominant type, and how to understand the strengths and weaknesses of other types.

PERSONALITY PROFILE

STRENGTHS

	Popular Sanguine	Powerful Choleric	Perfect Melancholy	Peaceful Phlegmatic
1	☐ Animated	☐ Adventurous	☐ Analytical	☐ Adaptable
2	☐ Playful	☐ Persuasive	☐ Persistent	☐ Peaceful
3	☐ Sociable	☐ Strong-willed	☐ Self-sacrificing	☐ Submissive
4	☐ Convincing	☐ Competitive	☐ Considerate	☐ Controlled
5	☐ Refreshing	☐ Resourceful	☐ Respectful	☐ Reserved
6	☐ Spirited	☐ Self-reliant	☐ Sensitive	☐ Satisfied
7	☐ Promoter	☐ Positive	☐ Planner	☐ Patient
8	☐ Spontaneous	☐ Sure	☐ Scheduled	☐ Shy
9	☐ Optimistic	☐ Outspoken	☐ Orderly	☐ Obliging
10	☐ Funny	☐ Forceful	☐ Faithful	☐ Friendly
11	☐ Delightful	☐ Daring	☐ Detailed	☐ Diplomatic
12	☐ Cheerful	☐ Confident	☐ Cultured	☐ Consistent
13	☐ Inspiring	☐ Independent	☐ Idealistic	☐ Inoffensive
14	☐ Demonstrative	☐ Decisive	☐ Deep	☐ Dry humor
15	☐ Mixes easily	☐ Mover	☐ Musical	☐ Mediator
16	☐ Talker	☐ Tenacious	☐ Thoughtful	☐ Tolerant
17	☐ Lively	☐ Leader	☐ Loyal	☐ Listener
18	☐ Cute	☐ Chief	☐ Chartmaker	☐ Contented
19	☐ Popular	☐ Productive	☐ Perfectionist	☐ Pleasant
20	☐ Bouncy	☐ Bold	☐ Behaved	☐ Balanced
total				

WEAKNESSES

	Popular Sanguine	Powerful Choleric	Perfect Melancholy	Peaceful Phlegmatic
21	☐ Brassy	☐ Bossy	☐ Bashful	☐ Blank
22	☐ Undisciplined	☐ Unsympathetic	☐ Unforgiving	☐ Unenthusiastic
23	☐ Repetitious	☐ Resistant	☐ Resentful	☐ Reticent
24	☐ Forgetful	☐ Frank	☐ Fussy	☐ Fearful
25	☐ Interrupts	☐ Impatient	☐ Insecure	☐ Indecisive
26	☐ Unpredictable	☐ Unaffectionate	☐ Unpopular	☐ Uninvolved
27	☐ Haphazard	☐ Headstrong	☐ Hard to please	☐ Hesitant
28	☐ Permissive	☐ Proud	☐ Pessimistic	☐ Plain
29	☐ Angered easily	☐ Argumentative	☐ Alienated	☐ Aimless
30	☐ Naive	☐ Nervy	☐ Negative attitude	☐ Nonchalant
31	☐ Wants credit	☐ Workaholic	☐ Withdrawn	☐ Worrier
32	☐ Talkative	☐ Tactless	☐ Too sensitive	☐ Timid
33	☐ Disorganized	☐ Domineering	☐ Depressed	☐ Doubtful
34	☐ Inconsistent	☐ Intolerant	☐ Introvert	☐ Indifferent
35	☐ Messy	☐ Manipulative	☐ Moody	☐ Mumbles
36	☐ Show-off	☐ Stubborn	☐ Skeptical	☐ Slow
37	☐ Loud	☐ Lord over others	☐ Loner	☐ Lazy
38	☐ Scatterbrained	☐ Short-tempered	☐ Suspicious	☐ Sluggish
39	☐ Restless	☐ Rash	☐ Revengeful	☐ Reluctant
40	☐ Changeable	☐ Crafty	☐ Critical	☐ Compromising
total				
totals				